BRIGHT NOTES

THE GREAT GATSBY BY F. SCOTT FITZGERALD

Intelligent Education

INFLUENCE PUBLISHERS

Nashville, Tennessee

BRIGHT NOTES: The Great Gatsby
www.BrightNotes.com

No part of this publication may be used or reproduced in any manner
whatsoever without written permission, except in the case of brief quotations
in critical articles and reviews. For permissions, contact Influence Publishers
http://www.influencepublishers.com.

ISBN: 978-1-645421-28-3 (Paperback)
ISBN: 978-1-645421-29-0 (eBook)

Published in accordance with the U.S. Copyright Office Orphan Works and Mass
Digitization report of the register of copyrights, June 2015.

Originally published by Monarch Press.
Stanley Cooperman; Laurie Rozakis; W. John Campbell, 1965
2020 Edition published by Influence Publishers.

Interior design by Lapiz Digital Services. Cover Design by Thinkpen Designs.

Printed in the United States of America.

Library of Congress Cataloging-in-Publication Data forthcoming.
Names: Intelligent Education
Title: BRIGHT NOTES: The Great Gatsby
Subject: STU004000 STUDY AIDS / Book Notes

CONTENTS

1) Introduction to F. Scott Fitzgerald   1

2) Introduction to The Great Gatsby   24

3) Textual Analysis
    Chapter I   26
    Chapter II   31
    Chapter III   35
    Chapter IV   39
    Chapter V   44
    Chapter VI   49
    Chapter VII   53
    Chapter VIII   59
    Chapter IX   61

4) Character Analyses   64

5) Critical Review   70

6) Essay Questions and Answers   78

7) Bibliography   82

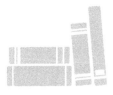

F. SCOTT FITZGERALD

. . . .

"Rich people," said Ernest Hemingway, "are poor people with money." It seemed to F. Scott Fitzgerald, however, that they were nothing of the sort, and he devoted a good part of his work to proving that "rich people" are indeed "different from you and me."

That Hemingway insisted upon reducing a complexity to some sort of manageable simplicity was totally characteristic of him both as a person and as a writer. And that Fitzgerald knew, perhaps all too well, that money was a crucial element in American culture, shaped the successes and failures of his work - and of his life.

THE 'CITY BOY'

Like Ernest Hemingway, Francis Scott Key Fitzgerald was born in "the provinces" of America: the Midwest. Unlike Hemingway, however (who was profoundly influenced by the great outdoors so much a part of his small-town childhood), Fitzgerald was born in a large city - St. Paul, Minnesota - and remained a "city boy" all his life. His family, moreover, was very much a part of St. Paul "society," and this too had considerable influence in determining the direction of his art, and the growth of his sensibility.

Perhaps one might say that it was simply a matter of a different sort of wilderness, but one thing is clear: if many of Hemingway's basic attitudes were shaped by his experiences hunting and fishing in the great North woods, many of Fitzgerald's basic attitudes were defined by the upper middle-class financial and social position that was his heritage.

Fitzgerald's maternal grandfather was the St. Paul merchant P. F. McQuillan, a hard-working man with the integrity and "soundness" so characteristic of the middle-merchant group of the area. Although the McQuillan fortune by no means belonged to the foremost rank of St. Paul money, the wholesale grocery business founded by the old man was worth over a million dollars at his death, and the McQuillan will left $250,000 to be shared by Fitzgerald's mother and the four other McQuillan children: two sisters and two brothers. That the McQuillan name was one of "substance" in St. Paul is indicated by the fact that Fitzgerald's own activities at Princeton, where he achieved a modest success as both a playwright and athlete, received considerable coverage in the society pages of St. Paul newspapers.

FITZGERALD'S 'SOCIETY' BACKGROUND

It was primarily due to his mother's family that Fitzgerald could be described as someone "born into the country club set." The family's position in this set, however, was rather ambiguous; neither "aristocrats" nor "nobodies," they dwelt in a kind of social twilight zone best symbolized by Fitzgerald's own description of one of the houses in which he lived as a St. Paul teenager: it was, he says, "a house below the average on a street above the average."

Such a position is hardly conducive to personal security, and perhaps helps explain why F. Scott Fitzgerald, while born into the exclusive "club" of the privileged class, spent a lifetime worrying about his membership - and worrying, too, whether the membership itself was worth the emotional and artistic energy he felt obliged (often in spite of his own better judgment) to expend in order to maintain it.

On his mother's side, at any rate, Fitzgerald was the inheritor of a tradition in which financial "success" was still defined by a strong awareness of moral solidity, an ethical responsibility, a tradition in which "good" business was directly related rather than irrelevant to good citizenship and social responsibility. It was, indeed, the kind of firmly based ethic referred to by Nick Carroway, narrator of Fitzgerald's finest work-*The Great Gatsby*-as he wishes for a world that would "stand at moral attention forever."

And the nostalgia for such a world was, certainly, to become an important aspect of F. Scott Fitzgerald's rather schizophrenic personal development.

A MORAL PROVINCIAL

Under the veneer of Princetonian aestheticism and despite his need for a "smart" identity (to be earned by "success"), Fitzgerald, in a very profound sense, remained a moral provincial; and it is precisely this moral "provincialism" - the nostalgia for moral qualities represented by the West and the scorn of the moral vacuum represented by the "East" - which is so basic to the dramatic structure of *The Great Gatsby*.

Throughout Fitzgerald's work, indeed, there is a tension between the pursuit of wealth (or an acknowledgment of the power of wealth), and a distrust of the wealth itself when it lacks the support of moral responsibility, and so becomes merely an instrument for the gratification of impulse. As such an instrument, wealth becomes destructive, and the American Dream-which is based on wealth-turns into the American Nightmare, the "Fitzgerald Woman" - with her charm, her parasitism, and her fatal lack of allegiance to anything but sentimental impulse (the gratification of which is made possible by wealth) -emerges as kind of child-Princess of doom, a "Golden Girl" whose very beauty becomes a form of vampirism.

The "solid" tradition of the McQuillans, however, was not part of the background of Fitzgerald's father-or rather, the tradition was of a different sort, at once more "romantic" and more vaguely defined. For Edward Fitzgerald's Maryland family could - and did - trace its kinship back to Francis Scott Key; and Edward Fitzgerald was himself something of a Southern gentleman whose manners were far more impressive than was his business acumen. Neither as a corporation executive nor as a broker was he particularly successful, and Fitzgerald's father remains a shadowy figure in the author's life.

Shortly after Fitzgerald's birth, on September 24, 1896, the family moved to Buffalo, New York, and lived for a time in Syracuse. After Edward Fitzgerald lost his job with Procter and Gamble, however, the family returned to St. Paul, and it was in St. Paul that Scott reached his adolescence. By this time both his parents were past fifty. His father seemed to become more "Southern" as it became increasingly obvious that his business career had reached a dead end, and his mother, having lost two previous children, lavished a rather baroque devotion on young Scott. The development of Scott as a "mamma's boy" was to shape many of his attitudes as an adult-a fact noted by many commentators on Fitzgerald's life and work.

The only other Fitzgerald child to survive childbirth was a girl, Annabel, but it was Scott who remained the focus of his parents' attention. Although details of Fitzgerald's early years in upstate New York are rather sketchy, the final portrait, as Kenneth Eble remarks, is that of "a somewhat pampered and sheltered boy, an occupant of apartments and rented houses, an inheritor of a sense of family superiority without much visible means to support it."

EARLY ADOLESCENCE

Back in St. Paul, the young Fitzgerald attended St. Paul Academy, where he demonstrated a growing affinity for literature. He published a short story in the school magazine, and kept copious journals. Even as an adolescent, however, Scott's attitude toward literature was ambiguous; writing, indeed, seems to have been merely one method among many for securing social status and "leadership," and Scott devoted himself with no less enthusiasm to club politics and athletics, not to mention "dancing class," as a means of achieving the status he so intensely craved even as a boy.

Reviewing his later career at Princeton, commentators have often wondered whether Fitzgerald's literary career would ever have come into existence had he been more physically suited for a major athletic career, or more emotionally suited for a sustained effort at campus politics. There is considerable justice, certainly, in the charge that for F. Scott Fitzgerald literature was a means rather than an end. Even as a schoolboy he felt no particular sense of vocation in literature, and his later career was to be seriously hampered by the fact that, for various reasons, Fitzgerald was forced to use his work as a key to open doors which otherwise would have remained closed, at least for him.

Such argument, of course, can easily be overstated; one can no more define the actual literature produced by Fitzgerald according to his motives in producing it, than one can define the prose rhythms of a writer like James Joyce through a mere description of his poor eyesight. What Edmund Wilson calls the "Sacred Wound" of the artist simply does not define the essence- or the value-of the art itself; and if the "Sacred Wound" of F. Scott Fitzgerald was a chronic inability to do his work for the sake of the work itself, one might also note that in this respect, as in so many others, his own conflicts represented the conflicts of his time and his culture.

In art, perhaps more than in any other field of human endeavor, personal weakness is no less a resource than is personal strength; the artist, indeed, very often uses his work to redeem the weakness itself-weakness which becomes, in a basic sense, a raw material of the art. It is true, for example, that if Ernest Hemingway had possessed greater social sensitivity and objective intelligence, his work would have been richer; but it is also true that the unique power of his work depended, to a great extent, on the lack of certain qualities which in themselves and in general terms are quite desirable. It would be foolish, after all, to attack Hemingway because he was not Henry James.

FITZGERALD AND LITERARY 'PURITY'

By the same token, to accuse Fitzgerald of having lacked certain elements of literary purity found in other writers, is actually to make a retrospective demand that he ought to have been somebody else. That he was not somebody else, is a fact for which readers ought to be thankful. Granted that Fitzgerald's weaknesses prevented his development along certain lines, they also created his development along others, and this is also true of writers like Hemingway, or Faulkner, or any other individual who sets himself the task of working words into literature. Given Fitzgerald's personal and social insecurities, one must indeed admit that he could never have written *A Farewell to Arms*. And given Hemingway's own fears and preoccupations, he could not have produced books like *This Side of Paradise* or *Tender is the Night*, let alone a novel with the unique value of *The Great Gatsby*.

It is possible, in short, to recognize that Fitzgerald's preoccupation with social status and "making good" took up much of his energy throughout his career, while also recognizing that the value of his best work is the result of precisely this preoccupation. And if there were certain qualities of adolescence and romance which Fitzgerald in his own way (like Hemingway in his) never outgrew, it was these qualities which provided the raw material for those Fitzgerald works which remain a vital contribution to American literature.

In 1911, Fitzgerald entered a Catholic boarding school in Hackensack, New Jersey-the Newman Academy, at which he spent two years. During this time he visited New York on several occasions, saw several plays, and continued his own apprenticeship in literature. He wrote several dramas, one of which was produced at school with Fitzgerald himself playing the lead: that of a very sophisticated "gentleman" burglar. And it was also during this time that Fitzgerald became aware of the glowing, romantic, and-for him-destructive power of sex, a power idealized into melodramatic sentiment, darkened by adolescent "disillusions," and surrounded by fears and distractions which he never completely outgrew.

THE FIRST ROMANCE

It was Ginerva King, a wealthy Chicago girl, who shaped his desire for - and fear of - the sort of "enchanting," careless, and essentially superficial female who was to reappear so often in his stories and novels: women like Rosalind in *This Side of Paradise*, or Gloria in *Tender is the Night*, or Daisy in *The Great Gatsby*-women who, despite their physical charm, are characterized by a profound emotional frigidity based partially upon a need for romantic posture, and partially upon a sort of instinctive calculation which leads them to use and exploit, and-when necessary-to discard their men rather than love them completely.

Fitzgerald actually met Ginerva after he had already entered Princeton; it was during Christmas vacation of 1915 that he began his "romance." The intensity of his emotion, however, was a source of embarrassment rather than joy for the young lady, who stopped answering his letters and ultimately married another man. Fitzgerald, deeply hurt, retreated into himself, and-as he so often did in times of adversity-retreated back to St. Paul as well.

A PERIOD OF DEFEAT

The next few years of Fitzgerald's life was a period of personal defeat and continued chaos. Forced to withdraw from Princeton because of the sordid matter of low grades, he spent nine rather aimless months at home, and returned to Princeton in 1916 trailing the rags and tatters of his various campus ambitions behind him.

The Princeton experience, together with the half-absurd bitterness of his relations with Ginerva King, his own background of semi-wealth, and his awareness both of the world of privilege represented by wealth and the changes wrought in that world by the impact of World War I (the moral and ethical loss of direction resulting from the impact itself), was to be rather lushly recreated in *This Side of Paradise.*

AUTOBIOGRAPHICAL MATERIAL

Autobiographical material, of course, was to be a vital element in the work of F. Scott Fitzgerald. Both his novels and stories-even such comparatively objective works such as *The Great Gatsby* or *Tender is the Night*-deal with his own experiences, or rather use such experiences as a focus for defining the enormous moral changes occurring in the United States.

Unlike many other writers of the twenties, who either "retreated" from America after the war, or attempted to objectify it through a broad-scope sociological analysis, or ridiculed it through **parody**, F. Scott Fitzgerald saw in himself precisely those aspects of "The American Dream" which had caused its own degradation. And for this reason the element of autobiography in his work is aesthetically and culturally valuable. "One of the most remarkable things about Scott Fitzgerald as a writer," remarks the critic Arthur Mizener in *Afternoon of an Author*, "is the dual character of his self-knowledge ... ":

The curious way in which he combined the innocence of complete involvement with an almost scientific coolness and observation, so that he nearly always wrote about deeply felt personal experience, and nearly always as if the important use of personal experience was to illustrate general truths.

So, too, the critic Alfred Kazin, in *F. Scott Fitzgerald*, comments on Fitzgerald's work:

[It] is full of precisely observed external detail, for which he had a formidable memory, and it is the gift of observation which has led to the opinion that he was nothing but a chronicler of social surface, particularly of the twenties. Yet, for all its concrete external detail, his work is very personal. The events of his stories are nearly always events in which Fitzgerald has himself participated with all his emotional energy.

F. Scott Fitzgerald, in short, did not "retreat" from America (either into art-for-art's sake, or the bull ring), and neither did he attempt any gradiose rendering of national culture. Using what he knew-what he himself had, either directly or vicariously, experienced before the war or in postwar America-Fitzgerald dramatized the dreams, and the illusions, which he felt to be at the core of America's greatness - and loss of greatness.

Like the Irish novelist James Joyce, who pledged himself to "forge, in the smithy of my soul, the uncreated conscience of my race," Fitzgerald focused upon personal experience which was indeed a microcosm of the experience of his nation. And in this sense, the work of Fitzgerald-while obviously "autobiographical" - transcends the personal, and becomes a dramatic symbol of human and cultural reality. His experiences at Princeton, his experiences with the fatal and parasitic "golden girl" who was to reappear so often in his books and who was to exercise so profound an effect on his life, his awareness of violently changing moral codes (which he was to regard with a mixture of fascination and repugnance) -these were vitally part of the development of American culture no less than they were part of the development of Fitzgerald as a writer and as a man.

THE PROBLEM OF WEALTH

Scott's preoccupation with the problems of wealth for example- with the central importance of money, and the dreams, the magical expectations, the carelessness," the ideals and the illusions which both create and are created by wealth - was certainly a very personal matter for him as an individual. As critic Malcolm Cowley remarked: Fitzgerald was like "a little boy pressing his face against a window, looking at a party to which he was not invited, and wondering who was paying the bills."

But this adolescent sense of exclusion, the vision of life as a "party" at which perpetually glowing men and girls achieved happiness-by-invitation, was essential to that adolescent Romance which Fitzgerald perceived to be at the very core of American "materialism," a uniquely romantic materialism which itself was the paradox, and the pathos, of American cultural development.

Fitzgerald's return to Princeton, at any rate, was short-lived; when he took up his academic pursuits for the fall term in 1917, Scott (like so many other young college men) was both distracted and delighted at the excitement of the European war, now America's war as well. His school career came to an end when he was inducted into the army, and the prospect of military adventure- together with his engagement to Zelda Sayre, a lovely Alabama girl of good family with a background of considerable wealth-seemed to offer some alternative to the emotional and intellectual drifting, the profound futility caused by his earlier failure at the university and by his previous relationship with Ginerva King.

ZELDA: FITZGERALD'S 'GOLDEN GIRL'

Both his hopes for military adventure and his hopes for a Supreme Love, however, seemed to collapse in rather ludicrous fashion: the war ended before Fitzgerald had so much as caught a glimpse of action (indeed, he never left the country), and his engagement to Zelda foundered in a welter of rejection slips. For after being discharged from the army in 1919, Fitzgerald had set about "earning" his Golden Girl by trying to write fiction while holding down a ninety-dollar a month advertising job. The magazines rejected his stories, and Zelda rejected Fitzgerald. There was a brutal simplicity to Zelda's action that Fitzgerald never forgot, and indeed, it provided a basic **theme** of his work: the **theme** of the delicate, lovely, and essentially parasitic woman whose affections - and loyalty - had to be "acquired" by success and protected by continued success, so that love itself, like a kind of stock-dividend, depended upon perpetual "investment" of emotional funds that were always threatening to be depleted.

Zelda herself, indeed, appears in many of Fitzgerald's works: in *The Great Gatsby*, she becomes Daisy Buchanan, whose voice "is full of money"; in *Tender is the Night*, she becomes the parasitic Nicole, first using and then discarding Dick Diver; even in *This Side of Paradise* such women as Rosalind or Beatrice Blaine (mother of the **protagonist**, Amory Blaine) prefigure the lovely but parasitic figures who are so fascinating and so deadly to Fitzgerald and his characters.

That Scott never forgot the manner in which Zelda broke their engagement is obvious not merely from his use of the **episode** in his fiction, but also from his comments in various journals and memoirs and letters. In one of these journals, for example, he vividly describes the "lesson" he learned from Zelda:

The man with a jingle of money in his pocket who married the girl a year later would always cherish an abiding distrust, an animosity toward the leisure class - not the conviction of a revolutionary, but the smouldering resentment of a peasant. In the years since then I have never stopped wondering where my friends' money came from, nor stopped thinking that at one time a sort of droit de seigneur might have been exercised to give one of them my girl.

The phrase droit de seigneur refers to the medieval custom by which the Lord of the Manor had the right to sample any bride about to be married within his domain; that Fitzgerald would use such a term to describe the woman he loved is itself an indication of how powerfully his imagination had been affected by the reality of money - and the fact that "Love," no matter how "Romantic," is very much a part of such reality.

Fitzgerald's comment is also very relevant to his work in that he makes a distinction between the "conviction of a revolutionary" and the "smouldering resentment of a peasant." For neither Fitzgerald nor his **protagonists** (not even Amory Blaine, despite his verbal gesture at radicalism which sets the tone for the rather pathetic conclusion of *This Side of Paradise*) really question the system itself. Awed by the power, the "magic" and careless grace of the wealthy, they do not challenge "the system" but rather occupy themselves with acquiring whatever baubles the system has to offer-baubles which indeed have a half-absurd and half-tragic importance because they become the only means of acquiring love, loyalty, and the chimera of imagined "happiness" - always "golden," always vaguely defined, always just beyond the locked fraternity door of some exclusive tomorrow.

After Zelda broke their engagement, at any rate, Fitzgerald quit his advertising job - and in his own word - "crept" back to

St. Paul to finish a novel, hoping to earn literary fame, financial security, and a wife, all at the same time. And he did just that.

THE BIG-TIME

It was, of course, a remarkable "pay off." When Scribners accepted the manuscript of *This Side of Paradise* in 1919, life turned into a Irish sweepstakes, with Fitzgerald holding all the winning tickets. Suddenly the "breaks" were going his way, and the Great American Dream of "striking it rich" had, almost inexplicably, become a reality.

The big markets-Smart Set, Saturday Evening Post, and Scribner's Magazine-accepted a total of nine Fitzgerald stories as though on cue, and after *This Side of Paradise* appeared in 1920 to mixed critical notices but immediate popular success, Zelda picked up her cue as well: she and Fitzgerald were married in New York's St. Patrick's Cathedral. The world, for F. Scott Fitzgerald and his enchanting wife, was a fantasy come true, a party where champagne and kisses flowed like money, while the American reading public payed the bills.

It cannot be stressed too heavily that Fitzgerald's courtship of Zelda was in many ways the vital experience of his life. The matter was actually quite simple: either he proved that he was a "success" and won the girl, or he did not prove that he was a success, and lost the girl. Money, in short, was the magic wand that would turn the land of ashes into a Golden Palace, and Zelda was a Fairy Princess with a price tag attached to each gossamer wing.

Fitzgerald himself describes the intense money-consciousness that filled his mind after his discharge from the army. Even his novel was an "ace in the hole" to be used for a poker game in which Zelda represented the stakes. "I was in love with a whirlwind," said Fitzgerald, "and I must spin a net big enough to catch it out of my head, a head full of trickling nickels and sliding dimes, the incessant music-box of the poor."

But Fitzgerald did indeed catch "the whirlwind"; the golden boy of American literature (he was in his early twenties when *This Side of Paradise* appeared) married his golden girl, and the year he and Zelda spent in New York (from the spring of 1920 to the spring of 1921) was a true-life fulfillment of "the infinite promise of American advertising." It was, as Fitzgerald later put it, the start of a "carnival" which was to continue for several years in Europe as well as in New York, a merry-go-round which, at least for a time, featured an inexhaustible supply of golden rings.

Despite its popular success, *This Side of Paradise* was rather churlishly received by serious critics, who saw the book as the work of a brilliant but generally unfocused talent. The structure of the novel is, of course, loosely episodic; provided with a minimum of plot coherence by the education of its "central" **protagonist**, Amory Blaine, *This Side of Paradise* was, as Fitzgerald himself remarked in one of his letters, a "picaresque ramble," and as such lacked either narrative or intellectual point.

THIS SIDE OF PARADISE

The very lack of a solid intellectual or social position, however, was itself one reason why *This Side of Paradise* seemed to dramatize so well the postwar mood of romance and futility, expectation and disillusion, "rebellion" and inconsequence. Reviewing the book in 1922, for example, the critic Edmund

Wilson (who was to become one of the most sensitive and perceptive of Fitzgerald commentators), remarked that *"This Side of Paradise* is not really about anything; intellectually it amounts to little more than a gesture - a gesture of indefinite revolt."

But it was the very "indefinite" quality of the revolt which made the book so appealing-the very naivete and lack of firm intellectual commitment even to rebellion captured a vital aspect of the postwar mood, a mood in which sex was often asserted without sensuality, radicalism embraced without ideology, and "success" worshipped without achievement.

Perhaps more important than the book's lack of intellectual substance was the fact that-as many critics were soon to remark-Fitzgerald himself lacked a certain objectivity in his presentation: he seemed, indeed, uncertain as to his own attitude toward his protagonists, and also seemed to assert precisely those values of romance and carelessness, of tinsel and moonlight, which sometimes, he attempted to mock.

The book, in short, seemed to be the work of a young man altogether too preoccupied with his own posture as writer, a young man whose imagination had been shaped by the vapourings of prewar aestheticism, and rather precociously "smartened" by postwar revelations and "new freedoms." Even in this respect, however, Fitzgerald was profoundly representative of his generation, a generation which, after all, had been a "Victorian" generation indeed, and had embarked on the Great Crusade of World War I - and the Great Hangover which replaced the crusade - with a singular mixture of bitterness and enthusiasm: qualities which themselves had been based upon cultural and intellectual naivete.

MONEY, MONEY, MONEY

Critical doubts notwithstanding, at any rate, *This Side of Paradise* began an enchanted period in Fitzgerald's life; a male Cinderella, he had achieved his Golden Princess - Zelda - and the two young people enjoyed their dream-come-true. Along with the parties, however, there were bills. Fitzgerald was actually living a frenetic life at this time, accumulating debts despite the explosive increase of his income, and turning out stories as though his typewriter were a money-machine. In retrospect, it seems almost astonishing that he produced some of his best short fiction during this time, and completed his second novel as well-*The Beautiful and the Damned*, which appeared as a serial in 1921 (in Metropolitan Magazine), and was published in book form in 1922.

Fitzgerald was to describe this period of his career as "the greatest, gaudiest spree in history," but, if his work is any indication, he himself sensed a core of rottenness beneath the surface of the splendor: a basic theme of his work was the futility, or rather the exhausting and febrile rush to nowhere which somehow seemed to characterize even the brightest promise of "success."

After a brief and largely uneventful trip to Europe, Fitzgerald and Zelda returned to St. Paul, where their daughter Frances was born; they then returned to New York, entered another round of the Gay Life, and finally rented a house in Great Neck, Long Island - an area which was to provide the setting for *The Great Gatsby*. Meanwhile the conflict between Fitzgerald's artistic hopes and need for money - and for providing all the baubles which Zelda demanded from life as a tribute to her existence-continued and intensified.

Zelda, said Fitzgerald later, "wanted me to work for her and not enough for my dream." It was not, however, that simple; the "dream" of F. Scott Fitzgerald, glittering with much false gold, was neither constantly nor clearly defined-even to himself.

THE GREAT GATSBY

In 1924, on the strength of a renewed production of stories and income, the Fitzgeralds went abroad once again, and this time the excursion was to last over two years. *The Great Gatsby* appeared in 1925, and although Fitzgerald himself felt that he had at last produced a truly important work ("My book is wonderful," he wrote to Edmund Wilson from France) the book received mixed notices from the reviewers, and-perhaps more important, at least in immediate terms-fell far short of the financial harvest produced by the two previous novels. Never again was Fitzgerald to strike it really "rich"; neither *Gatsby* nor *Tender is the Night* (his last completed novel, published in 1934) were best-sellers - an **irony**, of course, in the light of subsequent critical judgment.

But there was much justice to Fitzgerald's faith in *The Great Gatsby*, a novella of great symbolic richness and narrative economy, a morality tale of Idealism rendered pathetic and ultimately destroyed by a world in which Idealism itself is corrupted into random appetite and demands of materialism, while the face of "God" is advertised on billboards.

The Great Gatsby is not (and was not intended to be) a documentary study of social complexities or social abuses. The book is rather a lyrical rendering of a perception into American values based upon what Fitzgerald understood to be the central paradox of his own "biography" and the biography of his nation: a uniquely romantic "materialism" in which men attempt to create a glowing Ideal from material acquisition; in which - with no less "faith" than that necessary for any other mystic rite - they attempt to convince themselves that desire can define reality, that gesture can define action, and that sentiment can define emotion.

There is, in short, at the heart of *The Great Gatsby* - and of American materialism itself - a peculiar innocence, what Andrew Turnbull calls "the extraordinary gift for hope and romantic readiness," symbolized by Jay Gatsby as he builds his "enchanted palace" for Daisy Buchanan. And Daisy in turn represents what Nick Carroway, narrator of the book, terms "a vast, vulgar, meretricious beauty." It is the non-material or ideal quality of this materialism which makes of Jay Gatsby a perpetual innocent, a dreaming adolescent, a uniquely American Don Quixote tilting at windmills with a lance of gold, winning his Enchanted Princess, and counting his silk shirts as though they were rosaries. And there was, of course, much of Fitzgerald himself in both Gatsby and Nick, the latter expressing an affirmation (or perhaps one should say a nostalgia) for the traditional moral codes of the Midwest.

THE WALTZ SLOWS DOWN

Meanwhile, Fitzgerald's drinking had become both more intense and less "fun" than it ever had been. Long "rows" with Zelda ended in passionate reconciliations well-lubricated with tears and with alcohol, and while Zelda moved inexorably toward her mental breakdown, pursuing her own fantasies of a "career" in ballet and as a writer in her own right, Fitzgerald moved closer to the bottle.

Most of the years between 1924 and 1931 were spent abroad, and it was during this time that Fitzgerald became an intimate friend of Ernest Hemingway. At the beginning of their relationship, indeed, it was Fitzgerald who was the "established" writer and Hemingway who was the unknown; by the end of the decade, however, their roles were reversed, with Hemingway well on his way to a career as "The Champ," and Fitzgerald the "has been" writer whom Hemingway was to characterize so sharply in his story "The Snows of Kilimanjaro."

BOTTLES AND BREAKDOWNS

Much of the Fitzgeralds' time during these years was spent on the Riviera, although they moved across Europe from Paris to the sea with a restlessness which itself was born of despair rather than happiness. Zelda became more unbalanced, had one breakdown in Switzerland, and devoted herself to a short-lived career as a ballerina, while Fitzgerald found it increasingly difficult to work; a man hardly into his thirties, he was convinced that his career was all but finished. They returned to America in 1931. Zelda's father died shortly afterward, and Zelda had her second breakdown in 1932.

Living in Baltimore, while recuperating from her second attack, Zelda began *Save Me the Waltz* - an autobiographical novel which represented, she said, an attempt at a sort of self-therapy through work. Fitzgerald, however, saw the book in a somewhat different light. Zelda's motives, he wrote, were to reduce her husband to a "non-entity," to cut him down as a man of literature as she already had, in so many ways, cut down his manhood itself (and in this connection readers of Fitzgerald will find much fascinating material in Hemingway's posthumous *A Moveable Feast*).

While Zelda's condition worsened, Fitzgerald himself reacted to the shambles of his personal life by increasingly heavy drinking. He continued to work, however, and although his income had all but vanished, an important product of this period was *Tender is the Night*, written between bouts of illness, alcoholism, and all too obvious evidence that the condition of Zelda was becoming hopeless. After an attempted suicide, Zelda suffered her final breakdown in 1934, and entered the clinic at Johns Hopkins University. She was to spend the rest of her life in various sanitariums.

TENDER IS THE NIGHT

In many ways *Tender is the Night* is a recapitulation of **themes** already explored in *The Great Gatsby*: once again there is the "Fitzgerald female" (this time drawn along lines for which Zelda's illness provided much of the raw material), first using and then turning away from an essentially romantic hero ruined by his own idealism. Once again there is the "world of the rich" - a careless, ruthless world, the masters of which (like Tom Buchanan in *Gatsby*) are able to survive precisely because of their lack of sentiment. And once again there is the all-important **theme** of money, always so vital a force in Fitzgerald's imagination, and always closely allied with love and with sex itself. "Money," remarks the critic D. S. Savage, "here would appear in some obscure way to be the agent of feminine sexuality; by its means Dick, robbed of his male potency-the historical will to vocation, work, culture-has fallen into subjection to the natural female will to idleness and pleasure."

It is less, however, the "female will" that ultimately ruins Dick Diver, than it is the indulgence of impulse, a kind of "need" characterized by the lack of any will at all. Nicole, indeed, the "patient" whom Dick marries (and who exploits whatever strength he has to offer before turning, like Daisy Buchanan, to the brutal force and direction of an assertive lover), is morally incomplete because she herself feeds on the will of her man; ironically, it is precisely this flaw which finally insures her survival and "cure" in a world where moral will is a guarantee not of survival, but of destruction.

Dick, then, is ruined not despite his goodness, but because of it; in the moral wasteland those who give (rather than take) are simply drained and tossed aside, while morality itself, or the pursuit of ideal value, is associated with both weakness and impotence. Like Ed Wilson, who in *The Great Gatsby* makes the fatal error of actually loving; and like Gatsby, who commits the no less fatal error of devoting himself to an Ideal, Dick Diver in *Tender is the Night* makes the mistake of first rescuing and then loving a Fairy Princess of Money. The result is inevitable: he is, quite simply, consumed.

Tender is the Night received mixed critical notices in 1934, and although Fitzgerald remained the subject of some perceptive literary comment, he seemed to be a "dated" literary figure, of interest largely to a limited circle of those who had known him personally. After 1935 his work was thin, although the essays later edited by Edmund Wilson as part of *The Crack-Up* (which appeared in 1945) continue to be of great interest, especially with the resurgence of Fitzgerald's reputation in the last two decades.

THE END OF A SAGA

Despite an inheritance from his mother's death in 1936, Fitzgerald was deeply in debt, and worked in Hollywood partly in order to pay off his creditors. Illness, alcohol, and personal instability marked his last years; except for a continued close relationship with his daughter, and a rather poignant attraction to Sheila Graham, he seemed incapable of any sustained social contact.

In 1939 Fitzgerald began work on a new novel, *The Last Tycoon*, which he never completed. Although the fragment was extravagantly praised on its first appearance, critical judgment has tended to reinforce the impression that the continued emotional and physical exhaustion of Fitzgerald's life had taken its toll: *The Last Tycoon*-described by Fitzgerald himself as "an escape into a lavish, romantic past that will not come again in our time" - is something of an echo of the Gatsby **theme** (the "Dream" doomed by its own terms), but without the vital cultural relevance and narrative economy which make *The Great Gatsby* a major work of American literature, and without the retrospective control, the objectivity, which shaped *Tender is the Night*.

In 1940 the second of two heart attacks killed F. Scott Fitzgerald. Seven years later, Zelda Fitzgerald burned to death in a sanitarium. The saga of the Fitzgeralds had come to an end. The "failure" of Scott Fitzgerald, however, in all its pathos, its vitality, and its brilliance, had been the sort of "failure" that few writers achieve during their lifetimes.

Since Fitzgerald's death, critics and readers have come to see his work and his life as dramatizations not simply of "The Twenties," but of American culture itself. And from his very weaknesses, no less than from his strengths, from an imagination and romantic sensibility which-as Edmund Wilson has remarked-lacked "intellectual control," F. Scott Fitzgerald drew a portrait of his time which is also a definition of our time, and a portrait of his people which perhaps has more meaning today than ever before.

THE GREAT GATSBY

. . . .

THE STRUCTURE OF THE GREAT GATSBY

In *The Great Gatsby* Fitzgerald succeeded in achieving a certain "disassociation of sensibility" by structuring his book so that both the "Gatsby" part of himself and that other part-the firm part of his own moral and intellectual being-would complement rather than dilute each other. Using the device of a "dual hero" - that is, a first-person narrator who himself represents one aspect of Fitzgerald's moral vision, he created a work which is both more and less "autobiographical" than his earlier books.

If Jay Gatsby represents still another dramatization of the false dream of money which fascinated Fitzgerald throughout his career, it is Nick Carroway who represents an assertion of the traditional strengths which had made America great. By filtering the story of Jay Gatsby through the narrative of Nick Carroway, Fitzgerald not only defines what "The American Dream" had become, but what it could have been - and, perhaps, what at one time it actually was.

With *The Great Gatsby*, at any rate, F. Scott Fitzgerald produced one of the "small" masterpieces of American literature. Using the methods of impressionism and symbolic narrative rather than documentary **realism**, he succeeded in defining not only essential qualities of his own age, but in producing a tribute-ironic, perhaps, but nevertheless a tribute-to the basically idealistic vision of American material power. Whether this tribute must also be considered an **epitaph**, is not for us to say.

THE GREAT GATSBY

Very important to *The Great Gatsby* is the voice of the narrator, Nick Carroway, a young man of good Midwestern family who had "gone east" to New York for a career in stocks-and-bonds after serving in World War I. Nick actually narrates the entire novel, which is written in "first person": that is, the person of Nick himself. The fact that *The Great Gatsby* is "told" through the mind and personality of Nick Carroway is basic to the structure - and meaning - of the book.

THE MEANING OF NICK

Nick is far more than an "objective" or non-involved spectator; he is deeply involved in the action. For this reason, the reader must understand Nick while Nick comments upon Jay Gatsby and the other characters of the novel. In a very basic sense, *The Great Gatsby* is a novel with a "dual hero" - the story is "about" Nick no less than it is about Jay Gatsby, and both men ultimately emerge as moral symbols: Gatsby as the embodiment of spiritual desolation or waste, and Nick as a hope for moral and spiritual growth.

Ever since he had returned to the Midwest from the "East" and his experience with Gatsby, Nick has been attempting to define this experience for himself; the flash-back method of narrative employed by Fitzgerald is really a means to clarify Nick's own "education." For Nick Carroway is searching for a world in which some sort of moral code is possible, a world in which "conduct" and moral values involve something more than the mere gratification of impulse. Nick, indeed, remarks that when he returned to the Midwest he wanted "the world to be in uniform and at a sort of moral attention forever."

What Nick desires is a foundation for moral action, for he had found in the East - and in the person and fate of Jay Gatsby - only a "foul dust" of illusion, of "gorgeous" dreams rather than substance, of "gesture" rather than emotions, and promises rather than life. As for Gatsby himself: despite the fact that Nick despises his vulgar ambitions and schemes, there remains a pathetic tragedy about the man -pathetic because all of Gatsby's energy and "extraordinary gift" had been devoted to emptiness; and tragic because the very basis of Gatsby's idealism made its own degradation inevitable.

If Tom is at home in the world of wealth - his by inheritance and right - and uses it like the splendid and mindless animal he is, Jay Gatsby attempts to make of his own wealth a kind of magic key to a dream-palace of idealized bliss. This is a basic contrast: the fact that material wealth is, for Tom, what a toy is to a brutal and spoiled child; while for Gatsby material wealth is what a holy "vision" is to a religious mystic. For Gatsby, indeed, material "success" is itself an ideal, and this is the paradox at the heart of Gatsby's "romance." Tom, who uses wealth as he would a woman or a horse, survives through his materialism; Jay Gatsby, who would make of materialism a spiritual ideal, is ultimately destroyed by his own dreams. Nick's very first visit to the Buchanan mansion is highly charged with symbolic description and symbolic action.

SURFACE WITHOUT SUBSTANCE

The description of this scene is important because it introduces several **themes** or "motifs" of the novel. Basic to *The Great Gatsby* is Fitzgerald's rendering-through Nick-of a world in which appearance is not only mistaken for reality, but actually replaces it, so that the surface of things, or of people, rules out the substance of either. Nick, for example, tells us at the very beginning of the novel, that Gatsby's life had been "an unbroken series of successful gestures" - and a "gesture" is, by definition, the appearance of emotion without the emotion itself.

Throughout the book Fitzgerald reinforces this **theme** of "promise" that produces nothing, of "confidence" produced by fear (that is, the exact opposite of everything the word "confidence" implies), of "friends" without friendship, of "smiles" that are pasted on faces like labels on boxes of detergent, of "good times" that are manufactured like "caterers' productions," or "romance" without love, "pleasure" without enjoyment, "winning" without victory, "thrills" without consummation, and motion without meaning. Like the muscles of a frog that twitch to mechanical stimuli, all emotions are reduced to reactions, and all reactions are pre-packaged according to sentimentalized ideals.

THE FITZGERALD WOMAN

The essential coldness of both Daisy and Jordan is another basic **theme** of *The Great Gatsby* and indeed, Fitzgerald's work as a whole: that is, the view of American women as lovely, graceful, shallow, "romantic" but childishly selfish, childishly destructive, and-perhaps most important-emotionally frigid despite (or because of) their "romantic" and sentimental charm-a charm that is a gesture of life rather than a quality of living.

Fitzgerald very cleverly sets up a contrast between Tom's immense tension, his violence, and the awkward and bumbling manner in which he states his position-a position which (like all other positions in the novel) is little more than a **parody**: in this case of both politics and science. Tom's attempts to "talk," indeed, are parodies of intellect just as the "love" between Gatsby and Daisy is a **parody** of love itself.

DAISY AS ILLUSION

Daisy's voice, like Daisy herself, is an illusion, a "trick" which - as Nick understands - is little more than a device to "exact a contributor emotion" - or rather, the effect of emotion.

The as yet vague feeling that the world of the Buchanans represents some sort of moral rottenness, is reinforced by Nick's realization that Jordan (to whom he is physically attracted) is the Jordan Baker, a well-known amateur golfer. To Jordan, "victory" is a matter of mere appearance - a role to be played - and we come to understand that for her, as for Daisy, gesture has replaced internal no less than external truth, and illusion has itself become reality.

The result, of course, is that for Jordan Baker neither the illusion nor the reality is capable of providing true pride, or true satisfaction; hating the very idea of not "winning," she is nevertheless willing to obtain "victory" by means which make it impossible for the victory to have any meaning. And so Jordan too suffers from a kind of personal, almost spiritual hunger; a creature of illusion, she at once fears reality and yearns for it, and attempts to manipulate illusion in a pathetic and childish effort to secure the satisfaction of reality without its bothersome details.

THE APPEARANCE OF GATSBY

Very important in defining the basic **themes** of *The Great Gatsby* is the fact that Nick's first view of Gatsby himself is a peculiar one: the latter seems almost to be engaged in some sort of mystic rite, and Nick actually continues on home without speaking to him. For as Nick watches, Gatsby turns toward the Buchanan mansion across the bay-where a single green light gleams on the Buchanan dock. Slowly he stretches out his hands to the green light, in a gesture like that of a worshipper before a shrine. And then he vanishes, leaving Nick alone in the "unquiet darkness." And indeed Gatsby is a worshipper before a shrine: for we discover (as the novel progresses), that his shrine-and-Goddess is Daisy Buchanan; Gatsby is a worshipper of, and a pilgrim to, a vaguely realized image of some "beauty" which in truth is a mere vacuum.

THE GREAT GATSBY

CHAPTER II

Vital to the majestic structure of *The Great Gatsby* is the introductory descriptive passage in chapter II, which contains one of the most memorable images in the fiction of F. Scott Fitzgerald: a landscape of desolation over which presides - like a squat and obscene **parody** of God - the billboard face of Doctor T.J. Eckleburg.

Critics have made much of this scene, and with good reason. Travelling through the "valley of ashes," Nick is, in a basic sense, travelling through an inferno of the Damned - an inferno which exists side-by-side with the white and unreal dream of Gatsby's Fairy Princess-Daisy herself. And while Jay Gatsby (as the reader later discovers) is incapable of recognizing the "ashes" of what Daisy represents -and indeed, takes the emptiness for substance, and the ashes for some jewel of ultimate value - Nick Carroway sees all too clearly the spiritual desolation of the Buchanan world, and the tragedy so inevitable when Gatsby attempts to find in this world "the stuff that dreams are made of."

Even the colors of this landscape are echoes of Daisy: the "yellow" of Doctor Eckleburg's spectacles, the "yellow" brick of the houses on the street where Tom's mistress - Mrs. Wilson - makes her home. The color yellow, of course, is one of decay - but it is also one of riches as well: the color of sunlight and gold. And just as the gray dust of Doctor Eckleburg's landscape relates to the white "purity" of Daisy, so too does the yellow of Mrs. Wilson's street relate to the sordid and empty reality of Gatsby's dream.

In the Wasteland, it is people like Tom Buchanan and Mrs. Wilson, "consumers" in the most appalling sense of the word, who survive: feeding upon the dreams, the sentiments, or the fears of other human beings, they move like profane machines of flesh, using and breaking, and discarding all that gets in their path.

That George Wilson is to be the instrument of Jay Gatsby's destruction is one of the chief elements of structural symmetry in Fitzgerald's novel. For Wilson has this in common with Gatsby: neither is defined solely in terms of appetite or impulse. And in the world of the Buchanans and Mrs. Wilson, appetite and impulse-the gratification of ego or flesh-become the sole values of existence. Any remnant of idealism, no matter how diluted by a misguided worship of material surface, and any remnant of human love, personal commitment, or moral pride, is-in the Wasteland-a source of weakness rather than strength.

WILSON AND GATSBY

If Wilson is, as Tom says, "dumb" because of his love for and faith in his wife, so too is Jay Gatsby "dumb" in his idealization of Daisy. But while both men are wrong in their ideals, and are ultimately destroyed by the Ideal itself, it is precisely their mistakes which cause them to emerge as individuals finer, and more human, than those who survive them: In a basic sense, then, Jay Gatsby and Gorge Wilson are "balanced" against Daisy, Tom Buchanan, and Myrtle Wilson: on one side the echo-distorted, perhaps, and cheapened, but still vaguely (and helplessly) fine-of the old ideals of devotion and giving; on the other side, a process of mere taking, of "genteel" or vulgar consumption.

It is indeed the cry of "I want" that defines both Myrtle and Tom-the "I want" of an insatiable infant, picking up and breaking and throwing a way according to the impulses without emotion, and desire without meaning.

That both Gatsby's ideal and Myrtle's impulse are equally futile, is a clue to the essential tragedy of Gatsby's dream - and the "American Dream" itself, which, represented by Gatsby, is a Golden Palace built either on a dung-heap or a mountain of cotton-candy.

Nick, of course, who represents the "Midwestern" aspect of Fitzgerald's vision, is all too aware of the moral vacuum in which he finds himself-a world of verbal gestures, of false "ecstasies" and shallow opinion. The fact that he is not quite sober is actually a rather clever narrative device: since the scene is viewed through his point of view (as narrator), the result is both a heightened sensitivity and blurred impressionism which contributes to the effect, and the ludicrous horror, of this small scene of "The Wasteland" in action.

The very conversation in Myrtle's apartment serves as ironic definition of the sentimental but essentially destructive and parasitic "romance" of Daisy Buchanan herself - and of the "Fitzgerald Woman" in general. Myrtle of course, like other citizens of the Wasteland, reacts to appearance only; for her too, surface has replaced substance, the "suit" indeed "makes the man" - and one is reminded of the lines by the poet T.S. Eliot: "We are the hollow men, we are the stuffed men, head-pieces filled with straw...." That George Wilson, however, is indeed a "gentleman" or, rather, the emptied shell of one, is what sets up his own tragedy and the tragedy of Jay Gatsby.

A CRESCENDO OF BLOOD

Like all of the "good times" in the world of the moral Wasteland, Myrtle's party ends in disaffection and violence-a Walpurgisnacht of sordid and drunken unreality.

THE GREAT GATSBY

CHAPTER III

A deservedly famous section of *The Great Gatsby* is Chapter III, for in this brief account of the Gatsby "parties" Fitzgerald defines not only Jay Gatsby as an individual, but the perverted idealism and pathetic optimism of "the American Dream" itself. It is with this chapter too that the **imagery** of "enchantment" and unreality so basic to the novel is clarified: the **theme** of illusion and inevitable failure-inevitable because any illusion taken for reality contains the seeds of its own destruction.

THE ENCHANTED PALACE

Crates of oranges and lemons arrive before the weekend, and crates of pulpless halves-the assorted garbage of Gatsby's "productions" - leave after each weekend is over; and there is something almost obscenely ludicrous in the very juxtaposition of crates filled with fruit and cars filled with people-both consumed and discharged like the raw-material and end-product of some gigantic, meaningless digestive tract.

Nothing, somehow, is fixed to any sort of reality; there is laughter without amusement, "enthusiasm" between strangers, a disembodied and baroque celebration of some nameless holiday that had never occurred - and never will. And the guests themselves (most of whom Gatsby had never seen) act as though they were in "an amusement park" - a Coney Island for adults. The pathos, of course, is that for these adults - as for Gatsby - the "Coney Island" represents the only "high" life they know; it is indeed (as Nick remarks) a "simplicity of heart" and vague expectation, or hope, that is always waiting for some sort of ecstatic fulfillment - and always disappointed when the caterers depart, and all the golden coaches become once again the sordid pumpkins of reality.

TOURING THE "CATERER'S PRODUCTION"

When the gentleman calls Gatsby "a regular Belasco" (referring to a famous theatrical producer) the result is a definition of the entire Gatsby world: a theatricalism calculated solely for effect, a gigantic and somehow absurd (and perhaps touching in its absurdity) gesture of "the good life." It is all an elaborate "backdrop," a piece of stage-machinery against which Jay Gatsby plays out the tragicomic masquerade of his own dreams.

THE GATSBY SMILE

Nick's description of Gatsby at this point is very important. For one thing, it reinforces our awareness of Gatsby as not only a "producer" of elaborate and meaningless theatrical effects, but as being, in his own person, no less an "effect" than his pseudo-gothic mansion or unused books. Gatsby, in short, has in a basic sense "created" his own identity from personal romanticism based on socially pre-packaged labels; so completely does he carry out the ritualistic surface of the role he has created for himself, that the role ultimately replaces the self, and there is nothing left of Gatsby at all but the "act" of what he wishes to become.

The Gatsby smile, one should note, "builds" and grows more radiant, more intense, as though it were leading to a **climax** ... that quite simply never occurs. And this too is a basic quality of the Gatsby dream, the Gatsby romanticism (and the romanticism of the American dream itself). Always there is process without consummation, the gradual inflation of a huge, glowing, balloon of hope, or expectation, or ecstasy, until the balloon itself is suddenly punctured for one reason or another, and flops down to earth. And then there is nothing to do but wait for another balloon-if one has any breath left, or if the supply of ballons has not been exhausted.

GATSBY'S ISOLATION

Amid all the "Coney Island" celebration, indeed, Gatsby is a remote and almost "pure" - or at least, self-contained figure; and once again we have the clear impression that for Jay Gatsby the baroque "good times" he makes available for others is little more than a means to an end - an end involving some sort of Ideal that transcends, in an urgent yet undefined manner, the "good times" themselves.

JORDAN AND NICK

Sensing the core of honesty and moral firmness in Nick (who himself represents the old traditions of "conduct" and ethical responsibility, just as Gatsby represents a new world of moral expediency and false dreams), Jordan realizes that it is only with a man like Nick that she would be able to "go her own way." Nick, indeed, would always be there to pick up the pieces of whatever mess Jordan has made.

For Jordan Baker, in short, her "love" for Nick is simply one more calculation among many. Like Daisy and Tom Buchanan, she neither desires nor needs to be "careful" of anything or anyone; if the Buchanans rely on their money as a means of achieving what might be called freedom of impulse, Jordan understands that with a man like Nick Carroway she would achieve the same privilege. And Nick, infatuated with Jordan's beauty and charm, almost succumbs, That he ultimately does not succumb, is one of the essential differences between his nature and that of Jay Gatsby; drawing on the Midwestern traditions which both bind and protect him, Nick has the basic "soundness" which enables him to "go back home." For Nick Carroway is only an observer of the world of infernal enchantment. He has not become one of its inhabitants, and for this reason (protected by the bulwark of his own moral traditions) he can finally escape from the arms of even the most charming demon of the moral Inferno itself.

THE GREAT GATSBY

. . . .

GATSBY'S "NON-MATERIAL MATERIALISM"

When Gatsby calls for Nick one morning in his "gorgeous" car, one notes that the automobile has a very special meaning indeed. Like all of Gatsby's possessions, it is far more than a material object; it is a "sign" of the pathetic mystique which serves Gatsby-the representative of "The American Dream" - as he worships a kind of Ultimate Value that far transcends any material object at all. Gatsby's attitude toward material objects, again, differs sharply from the fleshly materialism of a man like Tom Buchanan; for Gatsby the material world is somehow elevated to a spiritual dimension, and the acquisition of material objects becomes almost a religious ritual. This is precisely what sets up Gatsby's ultimate doom: the fact that his "materialism" is itself a romantic "faith" in a kind of vaguely glowing perfection which the material world can never offer.

For Jay Gatsby, in short, "materialism" is itself an ideal, a romantic dream of unnamed spiritual ecstasy, a perpetual expectation which somehow turns to ashes when the "object" (whether a car, a mansion, or a woman) is actually achieved. In this respect he resembles another famous character of American fiction written during the twenties: the celebrated Babbitt of Sinclair Lewis' novel. Both Babbitt and Gatsby are caught up in a self-destructive paradox: they attempt to make spiritual affirmations of material things, and in the process find themselves with neither the spiritual dimension nor the values of materialism itself. Just as Babbitt makes of his office a "business cathedral" (and so degrades one and is disaffected with the other), so Jay Gatsby attempts to make of his cars, and his mansion, and his "silk shirts," and his dream of Daisy Buchanan, an act of worship. It is this "non-material materialism" which sets up Gatsby's ultimate destruction.

The car itself is described with an interesting series of adjectives-adjectives which communicate a sense not only of opulence, but of combined brittleness and softness, almost of decay. And Gatsby himself is emotionally infected with a perpetual restlessness, a kind of insistent disaffection or impatience. Whatever wealth has brought to Jay Gatsby, one thing is clear: it has brought him neither peace nor any real pleasure.

ILLUSION INTO REALITY: GATSBY'S SELF-HYPNOSIS

Gatsby's "autobiography" is memorable for something far more important than its elaborate falsehood. The significance of his manufactured "identity" is not simply that it is untrue, but rather that Gatsby has been attempting-with all the means at his disposal-to convince himself that what he knows to be false is actually true. He is, in short, involved in a sort of self-hypnosis; given the "right" stage-props, the right surface and facade, it is indeed possible for Gatsby to "double-think" himself into a kind of perverted "faith" in an ideal Jay Gatsby. That this ideal never in fact existed makes no difference; armed with stage-props and rituals, Gatsby is indeed (as Nick later remarks) trying to "fulfill his Platonic conception of himself."

So completely has Gatsby surrounded himself with the appearance of his own ideal, that he almost believes in it himself. Left to his own resources, however, Gatsby cannot complete the magical metamorphosis; the "conjurer's trick" he is attempting requires something more than his own faith in the "trick" itself. What it requires is the faith of others; not until he arranges the illusion so that it becomes reality in the minds of other human beings, can Gatsby rest secure in his own fantastic re-creation of life. Once other people "believe" him, the magic can indeed turn lead into gold - but first he requires that the image he has created be reflected from other heads.

Gatsby, in short, lives in a world of mirrors, a world in which illusion can become reality only if the transformation is publicly acclaimed; reality, indeed, thus becomes external rather than internal, and "anything goes" - anything is "possible" if private desire can be manipulated into public assent.

THE FRAGILE "ENCHANTMENT"

The problem, of course, is that false identities do depend essentially on externals, and the result is personal vacuum. Combined with Gatsby's optimistic "faith" that every desire can be turned into reality with the right stage-props, with the right gestures or "productions," there remains the nagging fear, the inevitable panic resulting from the fact that the "enchantment" itself can last only so long as the external appearance remains intact. Given any change in external circumstances; given any sudden eruption of crisis, or intrusion of real emotion, and the entire edifice must collapse; the "enchantment" fades away like cheap neon light, and the result is ... nothing at all.

There is no room, in an Enchanted Palace, for the sordid demands and necessary commitments of reality, and it is for this reason that Gatsby's protection of Daisy at the end of the novel represents something far more profound than chivalry; in protecting his Ideal, he is literally fighting for his own survival. For Jay Gatsby has so "enchanted" his own vision that without the enchantment he quite simply does not exist. Defined by externals, there is nothing beneath the surface; without his "faith" in material acquisition-the stage-props-as a means of securing his enchanted ideal, his glowing "promise," there is nothing but the Valley of Ashes, with the yellow eyes of Doctor Eckleburg peering over a desolated landscape from which all the fairy-girls and golden hosts have long since fled.

That Gatsby does have the Ideal, however, at once defines his non-reality and somehow redeems it as well, for it is by means of the Ideal that Gatsby transcends his own materialism-unlike the merely gross flesh of a Tom Buchanan. And it is for this reason that Nick, despite the fact that he finds Gatsby absurd and even offensive, nevertheless remembers the "purity" of Gatsby himself; the peculiar innocence and child-like hope, the sense of wonder that Gatsby radiates even in his complete inability to distinguish between truth and falsehood, between the real and unreal.

GATSBY AND DAISY

A creature of "whiteness" indeed, Daisy is the "fairy girl" of Gatsby's dreams in more ways than one - and her essential lack of emotion provides an important link in the chain of perverted "Ideals," pathetically futile gestures, and sordid circumstances that finally destroy Gatsby and his dreams. Gatsby's relationship with Daisy in this matter, it must be emphasized, resembles Fitzgerald's own relationship with his "fairy girl" of real life: Zelda, who was to be both his wife and his despair, and whose love he had to "earn" with "success." As we have already noted in our introduction to *The Great Gatsby*, Fitzgerald knew all too well the power exerted by wealth or the appearance of "success" even on the hearts of sweet young girls and the "romance" of love; the ironic relationship between money, now matter how achieved, and the Ideal of Beauty is a basic **theme** of his work and a basic comment on American culture as Fitzgerald saw it.

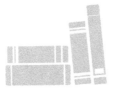

THE GREAT GATSBY

CHAPTER V

Once Nick understands the Gatsby-Daisy relationship, he (and the reader) also understands that Gatsby's entire "production" is aimed at the winning of an ideal, and there is a marked increase in urgency when Nick discovers the entire area of West Egg ablaze one evening with "unreal" light. It is Gatsby's mansion, where the lights have been turned on in every room. This is a very effective image, an example of the narrative economy of Fitzgerald at his best. For the blaze of "unreal" light communicates both the intensity of Gatsby's emotion, and the illusion which is the basis for the emotion itself. Some sort of **climax** is obviously in the offing - and if this climax turns into a absurdity, into an anti-climax of pathetic tragedy (as indeed it will), the cause is to be found in the nature of Gatsby's dream - a dream which (as we have so often remarked) contains the inevitability of its own destruction.

GATSBY'S GRATITUDE

The resources of Gatsby himself are so completely without a standard of either moral code or social perception, that his attempt to express himself becomes little more than a vulgarity. For in sincerely wanting to "thank" Nick, he offers to cut him in on a lucrative stock deal.

Under the circumstances, however, Nick has no choice but to refuse Gatsby's offer - for the offer itself would turn an act of friendship into a "business deal," and so become an act of degradation. That Nick perceives this, and Gatsby does not, defines the gulf separating a world in which all of human emotion - love or friendship, or gratitude - is little more than "business" and material acquisition, from a world (Nick's world of the Midwest) where there are still areas of human life which are simply not to be bought or sold.

The point to remember is that Gatsby does not mean to be sordid or insulting; he is using the only means at his disposal-the only "magic" he has at his command: material acquisition. It is, indeed, the same "magic" with which he hopes to achieve his Ideal of Beauty: Daisy Buchanan.

"GRAND PASSION" AND LOW COMEDY

Nick tries to comfort him, and finally becomes impatient: "You're acting like a little boy," he says to Jay Gatsby, the Prince of the Golden Palace, and this single remark defines much of Gatsby's peculiar charm - and pathos. For Gatsby, despite (or because of) his wealth, and his dreams, is indeed a "little boy" - a worshipper of toys which he takes to be signs of Divinity. For boy-men like Jay Gatsby, the trivial must be always elevated to the Cosmically Significant, and it is precisely this quality of "boyish" idealization demonstrated by Gatsby, that other American writers (Ernest Hemingway, for example) came to see as the unique "charm" - and maddening weakness - of so many of their countrymen.

THE PALACE OF ENCHANTMENT

And how does Gatsby react to the fact that he has at last captured his Butterfly Queen with a "net of gold"? He simply moves like a man sleep-walking through a dream that has suddenly become flesh. His very possessions, accumulated with such effort, suddenly become almost "unreal" in Daisy's presence; and indeed they are important only as they succeed or fail to succeed in giving her delight.

It is important to note, however, that the very realization of Gatsby's dream has in some way "spoiled" the dream itself; at this moment which he had idealized for so long, when his emotion is at "an inconceivable pitch of intensity," Gatsby somehow is beginning to feel a loss-a loss of something he cannot name or identify. "He was running down like an overwound clock," Nick observes - and the image, with all its absurd deflation, is indeed a description of Gatsby's ultimate fate.

GATSBY'S MAGIC SHIRTS

Gatsby's silk shirts as many critics have noted, are actually far more important than any mere garment ever spun by machine or man. For these shirts, to Jay Gatsby (like his car or his mansion), are important not in themselves, but for what they represent - and what they represent is the shrine of "success" and Ideal value made possible by success itself. Gatsby does not merely "wear" these shirts; he worships them, or uses them as sacred objects in a ritual whose meaning is, paradoxically enough, spiritual rather than materialistic.

To Tom Buchanan, for example, a shirt, even a silk shirt, would be-quite simply-a shirt. For Jay Gatsby the material object transcends itself; it becomes a mystic sign and spiritual endowment. This is what Daisy senses in this memorable scene-for as Gatsby continues to pile the rainbow of silk cloth higher and higher, Daisy literally collapses in a kind of ecstatic moaning; bending her head into the shirts, she begins to cry "stormily," declaring their beauty with sobs of mingled delight and sadness: like a music lover rhapsodizing over a violin solo by Bach.

The meaning of Gatsby's shirts, in other words, despite the peculiar absurdity of the entire scene, is that of a man who brings to his Dream a preoccupation with materialism which in some way has been transformed into enchantment; hence the relevance of the dedication on the flyleaf of *The Great Gatsby*, the bit of verse from the work of Thomas Park D'Invilliers:

Then wear the gold hat, if that will move her; If you can bounce high, bounce for her too, Till she cry "Lover, gold-hatted, high-bouncing lover, I must have you!"

GATSBY'S "HYMN"

After what might be called the "ecstasy of the shirts," however, Gatsby's mood of exultation somehow darkens and returns to a lower pitch. For having shown Daisy his palace, having reached her at last-knowing that she will be his-there must inevitably be a loss of enchantment itself. Daisy's fascination for Gatsby, after all, had rested in large part upon her very unavailability; made available once again, turned from an Ultimate Cause to simply another possession, Daisy must suffer a considerable loss in status. Gatsby senses this, a "loss" to which Nick refers when, describing Gatsby's appearance, he remarks that "his count of enchanted objects had diminished by one."

"Enchanted objects," after all, by definition disappear when touched; and this is precisely the measure of Gatsby's success - and his loss.

THE GREAT GATSBY

. . . .

GATSBY'S IDENTITY - AND THE AMERICAN DREAM

At this point Nick's analysis of the Gatsby character provides a basic insight not only into the character of the namesake of the novel, but into "The American Dream" of enchanted "success." For the dream of the 17-year-old James Gatz-the vision of "a vast, vulgar, meretricious beauty" that in some way was Divine as well as merely materialistic, is precisely the dream of Jay Gatsby as a man.

The pathos, of course, is that the fevered dreams and hope for some iridescent and glowing "glory" that one might expect from a 17-year-old drifter possessed of a keen imagination, is precisely the dream of the adult man as well. The result is a kind of nursery turned into a cathedral; a world in which the fairy-stories of adolescence (themselves based on pulp fiction) become the sole motivation of manhood, and are given an almost spiritual sanctification because they are the only Holy Cause which James Gatz -and the world which shaped him - can offer to human aspiration.

From his adolescence, in short, Gatz - Gatsby had been pursuing the Holy Glow of some vaguely imagined "success," an "identity" gleaming like a mirage just over the horizon of tomorrow. The result is both complete romanticism and complete lack of any real identity at all; obsessed (as Nick remarks) with "a promise that the rock of the world was founded securely on a fairy's wing" and viewing his own identity through fashion-magazine spectacles, Jay Gatsby-the Prince of Enchantment-indeed "sprang from his Platonic conception of himself."

It is, however, a "Platonic Idealism" whose only means of self-realization is material acquisition at any cost; it is an identity founded on facade, and a "self" which depends for its very existence upon illusion. This is the core of the Gatsby paradox, and the paradox of The American Dream itself: a unique kind of materialism that55.................. in a basic sense never "grows up," that is elevated into a perpetual, adolescent, romantic, and spiritual value. And because Gatsby's materialism-like American materialism-is all of these things, the result must be destructive; when material goals are reduced (or elevated) to spiritual cotton-candy, they dissolve at the touch.

The smile itself, of course, is still another symbol of the vacuum beneath the surface of Gatsby's appearance. Representing not a state of emotion but a state of ambition, the "smile" is an instrument to be deliberately manipulated; it is a social weapon rather than a personal tribute, and as such is no more meaningful than are the bright, "perky" and vacuous "smiles" which so often infest college campuses on sorority-pledge day.

GATSBY'S APPRENTICESHIP

Cody, however, was taken in by the Gatsby smile-for he was himself a creature of emptiness, an opportunist whose wealth was based on certain "lucky" transactions in the mine-fields of Montana.

But Gatsby was, in some basic way, made of finer stuff than his "mentor"; a romanticist even as a youth, he had remained apart from the worst dissipation, and indeed had at this time acquired a dislike for liquor which was to last all his life.

THE BUCHANANS AT GATSBY'S PARTY

The guests at the party contribute to the effect we have already discussed: a kind of kaleidoscope of insubstantial "fun" and meaningless charm, together with a hint - and perhaps more than a hint-of nightmare or vacuum beneath all the colored lights and "perfect" moon.

Fitzgerald, all through this scene, introduces images which serve to reinforce the lack of substance in the Gatsby-Daisy relationship, and so delicately does he combine fragile "beauty" with absurd pomp, that the result is an indirect definition-or redefinition-of character.

IMAGERY OF GESTURE

For Daisy Buchanan, indeed, emotion itself is a matter of "gesture", and anything too real is likely to prove "offensive" in more ways than one.

THE BASIS OF THE GATSBY-DAISY "LOVE"

Daisy, in short, is "in love" less with Jay Gatsby the man, than with Jay Gatsby the "Knight Errant"; one might say that she loves the gesture which Gatsby has made, the "romance" of unrequited love and noble devotion. This attitude, of course, is itself a paradox, for in loving the gesture of Gatsby, Daisy must-inevitably-find the romance of the gesture dissolving if she ever gives herself to him in the flesh. That flesh is precisely what she does not want, is a basic **irony** of the book.

Gatsby himself, furthermore has no less difficulty in "loving Daisy as a woman. So completely has she been for him an ideal, a Holy Cause, that to accept her for a woman with a real life and a real past-a past complete with a husband and a child-is no longer possible. In a basic sense, Gatsby has not only idealized reality, but has replaced reality with the Ideal.

Gatsby's insistence that one can indeed "repeat the past" is an important clue to his essential adolescence - an adolescence which he has never outgrown. For Gatsby no less than for Myrtle Wilson or Tom Buchanan it is "I want" that must serve as a **theme** for living; the difference between them is that what Gatsby "wants" is based on illusion, on ideal, while Buchanan or Myrtle recognizes no ideal at all.

Gatsby, at any rate, does not "want" Daisy as she exists; he wants his Golden Girl, his Golden Dream of five years before. That this Dream has actually lived with another man for five years, and - even more intolerable - had actually borne a child by him - has no part in his vision. One cannot, after all, imagine a "dream girl" in a state of pregnancy. Gatsby, again, has devoted all his "magic" to an image which no longer exists; he is indeed watching over "nothing" - and this defines both the purity of his romanticism, and the pathos of his innocence.

THE GREAT GATSBY

TEXTUAL ANALYSIS

CHAPTER VII

· ·

DAISY'S LITTLE GIRL

The little girl's appearance is itself a finely wrought **irony**. For Daisy's relationship to her child is hardly that of a mother to a daughter; the role of Pammy in Daisy's life is all too obviously that of a "darling" little toy - a toy to be "played with" and removed by the hired help when its presence is no longer convenient. "You dream, you" cries Daisy to the little girl, and for Daisy Buchanan her child is indeed a "dream" - a mere shape or decorative object in her life, the echo rather than substance of emotion.

Daisy's emotions, of course, are completely superficial; indeed, her very praise of Gatsby (that he looks like a man in an advertisement!) defines the nature of her "emotion" - or rather, her infatuation with the entire gesture of "having" a love-affair.

A VOICE FULL OF MONEY

Daisy, of course, has been rather indiscreet; in the world of impulse, however, caution is itself vulgar, and Daisy is simply too much of a child to control her delight in her enchanting new plaything: Jay Gatsby himself.

The voice of Daisy Buchanan, says Gatsby in one of the most important sentences of the novel, is a voice "full of money." And we immediately perceive the truth of this comment-the key to all the "magic" of Daisy Buchanan.

It is all a fairy-story, a **parody** of some child's tale of enchantment grown more ruthless - and more dangerous-because of the absurd misdirection of power which resides in wealth itself. And if Daisy Buchanan is "the king's daughter" of some real-life myth, Gatsby is for Daisy the Enchanted Prince of some real-life **epic**; when crisis intrudes, and demonstrates all too clearly that the Princess is a creature of flesh, and that the Prince is neither royal nor enchanted, all the dreams must-inevitably-go smash.

TWO CUCKOLDS

Where Wilson is deeply hurt, however, almost physically ill because of his wife's betrayal, Tom Buchanan is merely angry, furious, like an overgrown infant deprived of "his" property. This is a vital difference between the two men, and is a basic reason why Tom will ultimately survive.

Wilson's "weakness" is precisely the fact that he loves his wife too deeply; for Tom Buchanan, on the other hand, "love" is itself a matter of ego and appetite, and if he is furious that

Gatsby has engaged the affections of his wife, he is no less angry that Wilson is planning to deprive him of a mistress. It is men like Wilson and Gatsby-men defined by emotion or Ideals-who are ultimately destroyed; in the Wasteland of modern America, it is the flesh-ridden "realists" like Tom Buchanan who accommodate - and survive.

THE RIVALS

This is not to say, however, that Tom does not care for Daisy-or, for that matter, for Myrtle Wilson. It is, rather, that his love is on a different level; incapable of loving (or hating) an Ideal, his very emotions are in a basic sense pragmatic: that is, realistic. Unlike Gatsby, who tries to recreate the world according to a dream, and unlike George Wilson, who is ruled by his emotions, Tom is rich enough, and "simple minded" enough-to hold only those ideals which are useful to his own position in life, and to ruthlessly eliminate any emotion which becomes a threat rather than a pleasure.

THE SOURCE OF GATSBY'S "GOLD"

The pathos is that while Tom has the "goods" on Gatsby, he has not really described him at all-for everything that Gatsby did, he did for the sake of his Golden Girl, his Dream of Purity and Enchantment: Daisy herself.

THE END OF A DREAM

The paradox is one which lies at the very heart of American culture: in attempting to achieve a Golden Dream of Idealistic

Beauty through the only means available to him, Gatsby represents a world in which means have become totally subordinate to ends, where "success" is the only moral reality, and where the end itself-the Dream-is by this very fact reduced to a **parody** of any "purpose" whatsoever.

That Gatsby's Dream is itself a pathetic illusion, is dramatized by the reaction of Daisy Buchanan-who suddenly finds that her Fabled Lover, her long lost Prince Charming, far from being "above" the sordid reality of the world, has spun his "enchantment" from the most sordid and most vulgar element of the reality itself. And so Daisy Buchanan "withdraws" from Gatsby, withdraws from the sudden smash of her romantic infatuation like a sorority girl in white lace avoiding a puddle of grease. Everything is over; everything, indeed, is "dead."

THE DEATH OF MYRTLE

The scene is a vitally important one, for two reasons: first, it demonstrates that for all of Daisy's love of "romance" she is actually far closer to the brutal selfishness of Tom Buchanan-the selfishness and carelessness of the very rich than she is to the Idealism of Jay Gatsby.

The second point of major significance in the scene is the fact that while Daisy and Tom draw closer together-while they "conspire" to destroy Gatsby himself-Jay Gatsby remains under the fatal illusion that Daisy is still "his" girl, his Fairy Princess. And this illusion-as foolish as it is, and as pathetic as it is-once again defines the paradox of Jay Gatsby both as a man and as symbol. For it is Gatsby the bootlegger, the man who has literally sacrificed his entire life to the pursuit of an ideal, and who has made of material acquisition a shrine for the worship of that ideal, who is ultimately the one who gives rather than takes.

All of Gatsby's vulgarity, in other words, all of his "materialism" and single-minded pursuit of wealth, has been, in a very basic sense, founded upon his willingness to sacrifice himself for that in which he believes: the Ideal Beauty to be achieved through work, and effort, and purity of devotion. It is Tom Buchanan and Daisy who, completely without ideals or any spiritual dimension, simply "retreat into their money" at any eruption of crisis.

Such is the nature of Gatsby's purity, that the "something" in him which Nick perceives as spiritual rather than material, leads him to self-sacrifice rather than to self-protection; all that he has done-all the evil that he has perpetuated-has been done not for himself, but for others-for the sanctification of his Dream. And this, of course, is a paradox not only of Gatsby, but-as we have indicated-of what sociologists and critics have termed "The American Dream" - a kind of materialism devoted to spiritual values.

A WASTE OF POWER

That Gatsby's spiritual value-his Ideal Cause-is the amoral sentiment and the random impulse of Daisy Buchanan, is itself the deepest horror of his situation. And this situation, again, is grounded not in "evil," but rather is wasted goodness: the goodness of devotion, in almost religious terms, to a "Goddess" made of tinfoil and rotten gumdrops. This **theme** of waste-a waste of devotion, a waste of human resources, a waste of ambition-is basic to *The Great Gatsby* as a novel. It is also a basic

BRIGHT NOTES STUDY GUIDE

theme of the work of Fitzgerald and of other American writers as well. From Henry James to John Steinbeck, from Mark Twain to Sinclair Lewis, American writers have been obsessed with the image of America as a power for good somehow diverted into an instrument of the false and the trivial.

Just so does Jay Gatsby, the pathetic, the vulgar, and yet - in some way - noble "knight errant," mobilize his own resources to "protect" his ideal: Daisy Buchanan. And it is for this reason that Nick Carroway remarks, while Gatsby "watches" over the Buchanan house (where, unknown to him, Daisy and her husband are "conspiring" for his destruction), that Gatsby is watching over "nothing" - a nothingness which is indeed the essence of the dream of Jay Gatsby, and perhaps the dream of American "Success" as well.

THE GREAT GATSBY

CHAPTER VIII

FLASHBACK TO A HOLY GRAIL

But something unexpected happened: instead of taking Daisy and forgetting her, he had found that she became, for him, a total definition of value - self-value no less than ego-value. He had begun to love Daisy like a man "committed ... to the following of a grail" and from that moment Jay Gatsby conceived of the mysterious world of wealth as itself a magical ideal of perfection and purity.

NICK'S JUDGMENT OF GATSBY

As Nick says good-bye to Gatsby, he senses the core of idealism at the heart of his vulgar ostentation and indeed remarks on the "incorruptible dream" shaping the nature of Gatsby's material corruption.

In the final analysis it is Jay Gatsby who tried to keep some sort of spiritual value alive in the moral "ashheap" ruled by the Buchanans.

THE DEATH OF GATSBY

Gatsby's death, like his life, is the product of an illusion; Wilson's death, like his life, is the product of misplaced faith and a love which-in the Wasteland-can achieve no greater dignity than hysteria.

THE GREAT GATSBY

....

FINAL EULOGY

The last chapter of *The Great Gatsby* actually serves as an epilogue, a final comment on the futility and emptiness of all that James Gatz-the dreaming Minnesota adolescent-had "succeeded" in accomplishing.

It is Gatsby's father, however-a bedraggled little man from a little town in Minnesota-who provides the final note of pathos. In New York for Gatsby's funeral, Henry C. Gatz sadly tells Nick that his son could have been "a great man." And indeed he could-given a different purpose to his life, or rather, given a world where dreams need not be confused with reality, and where material acquisition and material display need not be elevated into some sort of pseudo-spiritual "happiness."

GATSBY AS SYMBOL

For the central truth about Jay Gatsby was that he was a knight-errant devoting himself to a pilgrimage in which the only "Jerusalem" is the moral and spiritual vacuum represented by Daisy Buchanan; he was, indeed, a Sir Lancelot of **epic** resources, faced with a world in which the Holy Grail had been reduced to a blinking neon light.

THE "AMERICAN DREAM" WASTED

Self protection, like self-indulgence, is the only absolute commandment which the Buchanans, kings and inhabitants of the Wasteland, can possibly recognize. "Careless" with the power that comes with wealth; completely self-centered with the total egotism of moral primitives, people like Daisy and Tom "smashed things up...and let other people clean up the mess they had made."

RETREAT TO THE PAST

Ultimately, it is the "capacity for wonder" and devotion to an ideal which had made America great; and it is the loss of this "wonder," and the degradation of the ideal, which had turned the "green land" to the ashheaps of Doctor Eckleburg. Nick understands all too well that the story of Jay Gatsby represents far more than the fate of a poor boy who had tried to get enough money to marry his "true love." For the story of Gatsby is also the story of wonder, and power, and devotion, turned into instruments of a machine of false values, a machine which first spawns and then eats its own children, and exists for no other purpose than its own digestion.

Such is the world which had destroyed "Jay Gatsby" - a senseless arrangement of vulgar appetites in which motion has replaced direction, impulse has replaced moral choice, and "love" has become little more than a process of mutual cannibalism. And the tragedy of the book is that Nick's return to the Midwest is, in a profound sense, less a hope for America's future, than a retreat into America's past.

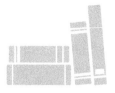

THE GREAT GATSBY

. . . .

NICK CARROWAY

The narrator of the novel, Nick, represents the traditional moral codes of America. Himself from the Midwest (which contrasts to the East of Long Island and the world of the Buchanans), Nick is attracted by the beauty, the wealth, and the sophistication of "The Wasteland" - but comes to understand the essential emptiness, the gaudy display of "nothingness" which characterizes the Wasteland itself. As the critic Arthur Mizener remarks, the novel is, in a basic sense, Nick's story as well as Gatsby's, for it is Nick who at last achieves a "gradual penetration of the charm and grace of Tom and Daisy's world. What he penetrates to is corruption, grossness, and cowardice."

It is Nick too who perceives the essential pathos of Jay Gatsby, the romantic idealism which shapes his very materialism, and so sets him off sharply from the gross and fleshly Tom Buchanan. Nick, indeed, who says that he wishes the world "to stand at moral attention forever," understands that Gatsby is motivated not by selfishness, but rather by devotion-devotion to an ideal rendered false by the appetites and moral vacuum of the Wasteland. Alone among all of Gatsby's "friends" (with the exception of the character called "Owl-Eyes") to pay a final tribute to the pathetic bootlegger-Idealist, Nick sees Gatsby as being a symbol of the American Dream gone sour, an "innocent" destroyed by a corrupt world. And when Nick leaves the East, he does so with the hope of finding some remnant of a moral and personal reality "back home."

JAY GATSBY

The "subject" of the novel, Jay Gatsby is a dramatic symbol of the Idealism which makes of materialism itself a type of romantic expectation-a uniquely American "non-material materialism." Gatsby, indeed, is a kind of pathetic "Don Quixote" tilting at non-existent windmills and counting his silk shirts as though they were rosaries; attempting to achieve a glow of vague spiritual "enchantment" through material acquisition, Gatsby represents the paradox - and the pathos - of spiritual values reduced to vulgarity and futility in the moral Wasteland.

The essential tragedy of Gatsby is, in a profound sense, the tragedy of American Idealism itself: the waste of enormous energies, even self-sacrifice, to self-illusion and (as Nick remarks) the service of a "vast, vulgar meretricious beauty." Gatsby, furthermore, has no means to communicate his Idealism, or fulfill it, aside from the false standards of the Buchanan world itself.

Perhaps the chief element in Gatsby's inevitable destruction is the fact that his romanticism, his misplaced "faith" in material success (as a kind of spiritual rite and proof of identity), is so intense, that he ultimately believes that he can indeed recreate reality according to his heart's desire. A "magician" in a world of sordid appetite and cowardice, Gatsby's "dream" is-by the conditions of its own existence-doomed to failure. For he cannot "regain" Daisy simply because he pursues her not really as a woman, but as an Ideal. And as an Ideal, Daisy Buchanan - and all she represents - must vanish like spiritual cotton-candy at the first eruption of crisis.

TOM BUCHANAN

The husband of Daisy and lover of the gross and fleshly Myrtle Wilson, Tom is both ruler and representative of the moral Wasteland which has replaced American Idealism. Tom is a creature of brute appetite and direct "action" based on self-preservation and self-interest rather than any idealism whatsoever. He is "strong" because in the moral Wasteland idealism itself is a source of weakness rather than strength; devoted to nothing but the impulses of his own flesh and the demands of his own ego, completely without any concept of either a moral code or personal loyalty.

For Tom and Daisy Buchanan there is no moral responsibility whatsoever; they "retreat into their money" at any crisis, and "leave other people to clean up the mess."

DAISY BUCHANAN

Gatsby's "Golden Girl," the dream and "Cause" of his wasted idealism, Daisy falls into a familiar pattern of Fitzgerald women. These women are lovely, delicate, and "romantic" - but essentially parasitic, and emotionally frigid despite (or because of) their sentimentality. Critics, indeed, have noted that Fitzgerald's attitude toward women is very ambivalent; perhaps because of his traumatic experience with Zelda, he combined an extremely romantic "worship" of them (much like Gatsby's) with an equally extreme distrust of them-a distrust which approaches actual fear.

Arthur Mizener, for example, notes that Fitzgerald "never loved merely the particular woman; what he loved was her embodiment for him of all the splendid possibilities of life he could, in his romantic hopefulness, imagine." On the other hand, a critic like Charles E. Shain notes the procession of "mercenary" and "fatally irresponsible" women in Fitzgerald's work-women who are "as dangerous to men as classical sorceresses." So too William Goldhurst notes that Fitzgerald imaged the American woman as "physically attractive," but having a "destructive influence on the man with whom she is associated."

Daisy Buchanan, motivated by weakness rather than passion, and by sentiment rather than emotion, is simply impelled by any force ready to determine her direction, and to protect her from either emotional discomfort or emotional commitment. The basic fact of Daisy is her lack of substance, and *The Great Gatsby* is filled with images which reinforce this emptiness, images which follow Daisy Buchanan through Fitzgerald's pages like the gossamer cloth "floating" around her face. Loyal only to sentiment and the gesture of love, she deserts Gatsby at the eruption of crisis like a sorority girl in white lace avoiding a puddle of grease.

JORDAN BAKER

Jordan is no less a creature of the moral Wasteland than is Daisy or Tom Buchanan. A "lovely" girl who (like Daisy) dresses in "white" and always seems to be "cool," Jordan is an opportunist

BRIGHT NOTES STUDY GUIDE

in her own way. Nick is attracted to her, but ultimately breaks up with her because he sees in Jordan that same ability for irresponsible exploitation that he sees in Daisy and Tom.

MYRTLE WILSON

Myrtle is one of the "users" of the Wasteland-just as her husband is one of the used. A creature of impulse (she met Tom on a train and just "had" to have him), she is blood-rich and full, loud and sentimental-with ludicrous mannerisms of borrowed "refinement." Myrtle too is a kind of parasite on the misplaced idealism of George Wilson, who appears and reappears in the novel like a man being slowly eaten by a vampire. It is symbolically fitting that Myrtle Wilson dies as she had lived: violently, with a gush of blood, killed by a car driven by Daisy Buchanan.

GEORGE WILSON

Myrtle's husband, a hapless shadow of what once had been a handsome man, George-like Gatsby himself-is destroyed by the fact that he holds to ideals of honor, and actually loves his wife. In the moral Wasteland, those with ideals and those who truly love are alike vulnerable, and it is ironically apt that it is George Wilson who shoots Gatsby before taking his own life. Like Gatsby, Wilson is, in his own way, a romanticist.

MEYER WOLFSHEIM

Wolfsheim is a memorable figure, and his very "sentiment" creates a kind of absurd horror-like modern "syndicate" gangsters who are "nice" citizens in their own community, and who contribute to boy-scout troops while controlling the sale of narcotics.

PAMMY

When Daisy calls her daughter a "dream" she is indeed defining her own incapacity for any sort of real emotion.

HENRY G. GATZ

Gatsby's father, who comes to New York for the funeral, and shows Nick the pathetic excerpt from Gatsby's diary - an excerpt replete with laudable virtues and Franklin-like resolutions. It is Mr. Gatz who remarks that his son could have been "a great man" - and indeed the waste of the resources of energy and idealism is a basic **theme** of the novel.

DOCTOR J. ECKLEBURG

Eckleburg's face, indeed, is taken by George Wilson as being "the eyes of God" - and this is one of the most memorable absurdities of the book. As an image, Doctor Eckleburg is extraordinarily effective; the monstrous face and yellow eyes become a **parody** of Divinity.

F. SCOTT FITZGERALD

CRITICAL REVIEW

"I talk with the authority of failure," F. Scott Fitzgerald once wrote in his notebooks, soon after his break with Ernest Hemingway, "Ernest with the authority of success. We could never sit across the same table again." Whether or not Fitzgerald considered himself a "failure" in his own lifetime, however, one thing is clear: during the last decade, his reputation among literary critics and non-specialized readers has grown to the point where no study of American literature - and certainly no anthology of American literature - is complete without either a discussion or representation of his work.

THE QUESTION OF FITZGERALD'S "FAILURE"

The question of Fitzgerald's "failure" has been to a great extent the result of two elements in Fitzgerald's career: first, the fact that he did produce an enormous number of "slick" stories for the high-priced magazines, while two of his four novels (*This Side of Paradise* in 1920, and *The Beautiful and the Damned* in 1922) were "best sellers" from a financial, if not literary point of view.

Fitzgerald, in short, was preoccupied with financial success throughout his career, and much of his work was indeed produced with the market rather than the muse foremost in his mind. As Arthur Mizener points out, most of the 160 stories that Fitzgerald wrote between 1920 and (approximately) 1940 were frankly written for money. For this reason, if for no other, Fitzgerald's critical reputation was indeed vulnerable; literary critics have always tended to look askance at undue financial success (or preoccupation) on the part of literary artists, a fact which is obvious enough in the careers of such writers as John Steinbeck and Ernest Hemingway among many others.

The fact that Fitzgerald did produce a great deal of semi-hack writing, and the fact that he became a literary celebrity too early and too richly in his career, undoubtedly shaped critical attitudes toward his work. In addition to this aspect of the Fitzgerald career, however, there was also the fact that he became so thoroughly identified with the glittering world of flappers, disillusions, and "early sorrows" romantically a part of the mythology of the American twenties, that critics often seemed to be rendering a judgment not on Fitzgerald's work, but rather on the cultural environment which provided its raw material. The news-columnist Westbrook Pegler, for example, summed up this sort of blanket dismissal by referring to Fitzgerald as being both spokesman for and representative of a "group or cult of juvenile crying-drunks."

It is always dangerous, however, to confuse the **theme** which a writer uses for his work, with the status or value of the work itself. A novelist like Virginia Woolf, for example, is not to be considered aesthetically "sterile" merely because psychological and emotional sterility is a basic **theme** of her books. And if "failure" is a basic **theme** of F. Scott Fitzgerald, one must remember that he was attempting to render a society which had indeed "failed" precisely because of its universal preoccupation with "success."

That Fitzgerald himself illustrated this paradox-a worship of "success" so intense that it virtually insures a conviction of personal failure-in no way invalidates his artistic vision. On the contrary, the fact that Fitzgerald was so completely a man of his own time and own culture, explains to no small degree his ability to render cultural reality in his stories and novels.

Fitzgerald was not invulnerable to the American Dream of "success without sweat"; ironically (and sometimes bitterly) aware of his own "mixed motives" as an artist, he saw in himself precisely those moral and intellectual flaws which were shaping the direction of America as a nation. Granted that he was extremely sensitive to his times, one must remember that such a sensitivity is hardly a disadvantage to a literary artist. That Fitzgerald possessed this sensitivity enabled him to use in his work what the critic Glenway Wescott has called an "extreme environmental sense."

EARLY WORK

In his early work, however, Fitzgerald seemed to have the "environmental sense" without the aesthetic objectivity which alone serves to shape literature into something more than a reflection of prevailing intellectual or social modes. Quite aside from the financial and personal necessities which drove him to "selling big" to the "big markets," one might almost say that Fitzgerald had been too close to "his times"; that he had not yet succeeded in viewing the times themselves - and the tensions within himself so vitally characteristic of them - through a structuring of fiction which would stand alone, independent of fashionable literary posture, or current intellectual preoccupations, or personal anticipations in which the writer almost seems to view his own achievement before the work itself has been achieved.

This Side of Paradise, for example, which made Fitzgerald something of a literary celebrity in 1920 (and which, of course, enabled him to "earn" Zelda and build his own Golden Palace of "success") was attacked by literary critics on precisely these grounds: that it was far too completely a "mixed bag" of assorted literary modes, prevailing intellectual "smartness," moral exposes which themselves indicated a certain naivete on the part of the author, and a certain sophomoric anxiety to "shock" as well as please. As Heywood Broun rather dyspeptically remarked of the book: "There is too much footwork and too much feinting for anything solid and substantial being accomplished. You can't expect to have blood drawn in any such exhibition as that."

THE NEED FOR OBJECTIVITY

Critics were generally agreed that Fitzgerald's own enthusiasm as a story-teller, his own romanticism as a person, his own delight in the "smart" and topical, his own view of literature as a kind of "key" to the "good life," and his obvious debt to those writers (such as Tarkington, Wells, and others) who had been fashionable among Princeton undergraduates, resulted in a kind of grab-bag of literary mannerisms. There was, in short, general agreement that while Fitzgerald might be a brilliant addition to the American literary scene, he was as yet what Frederick Hoffman called a genius manque-a rather precocious young man who seemed to be playing a "brilliant" role in some drama of his own creation, a drama in which the novel itself was merely an episode.

The need for objectivity in Fitzgerald's work, the need for less self-conscious play-acting at literature and "being in the know," was a criticism reiterated by literary commentators such as Edmund Wilson, Paul Rosenfeld, and many others. Certainly Fitzgerald's first two novels are marked by a lack of what James E. Miller, Jr. calls the principle of selectivity; still very much the bright young author, Fitzgerald in *This Side of Paradise* and *The Beautiful and the Damned* (although to a somewhat lesser extent in the latter work) tends to sacrifice control and structure to a kind of pyrotechnic display of random witticisms, social observations, fashionable comment (or condescension), irrelevant "self-expression" - all the flaws, in short, of a young writer impressed with himself and with the need to be "successful" at least as much as he is impressed with the art of literature.

THE CRITICS AND GATSBY

With *The Great Gatsby* in 1925, however, this structural control was achieved-achieved through both the dual narrative we have already discussed (the technique, partly influenced by the novelist Joseph Conrad, of filtering action and meaning through a narrator at once involved with the action and commenting upon it), and through the use of "natural" symbols growing out of the action and situation of the story: the eyes of Doctor T. J. Eckleburg, for example, or the "green light" of Daisy Buchanan, or the "ritual of the silk shirts" in Gatsby's mansion. The book, in short, was praised by critics as a profound definition of the loss of American values-the loss of "The American Dream" - and a work of literary art in which ironic drama was all the more powerful for being controlled and absorbed within the substance of the work itself.

It was not so much that *The Great Gatsby* was (as Andrew Turnbull remarks) "less autobiographical" than Fitzgerald's earlier works, as it was that the autobiography had been used more relevantly to the fiction. In posing the "Jay Gatsby" part of his own vision against the "Nick Carroway" part, Fitzgerald had achieved the sort of objectivity which makes it possible for a novelist to "stay out of his book" - or rather, to let the book say what it has to say without intrusive explication. There is less of Fitzgerald "talking" to his readers as Fitzgerald than in either of his earlier novels, and this is also true of what most critics consider to be the novel ranking next to *Gatsby*: *Tender is the Night*, which appeared in 1934.

The Great Gatsby, at any rate, was highly praised; William Rose Benet, for example, in a Saturday Review essay, remarked that "for the first time Fitzgerald surveys the Babylonian captivity of this era unblinded by the bright lights," and commentators such as Malcolm Cowley, Dennis Hardy, James Thurber, Edmund Wilson, John Peale Bishop, and many others sensed a new substance in Fitzgerald's work.

CRITICAL RESERVATIONS

This is not to say that Fitzgerald had achieved any sort of literary apotheosis or Sainthood. The critical voices were by no means unanimous, even on the subject of *The Great Gatsby*; H. L. Mencken, for example, attacked both the novel (which he considered little more than an "anecdote") and its chief character, whom he considered so "vague" as to be a sort of disembodied shadow of a literary **protagonist**. *Tender is the Night* received mixed reviews, and there remained much critical feeling that F. Scott Fitzgerald had indeed "wasted" too much of his talent on unworthy projects, while personal difficulties (his own and Zelda's) had wasted too much of him. So completely had the Fitzgerald reputation lost its glitter, that by 1939 the best of his novels- *The Great Gatsby* - was actually dropped from the list of Modern Library Editions because it 'failed to sell'.

FITZGERALD'S GROWING REPUTATION

After Fitzgerald's death, however, the tide shifted, and by the time Edmund Wilson had edited and published *The Crack-Up* in 1945, with serious critical essays, interest in Fitzgerald both as an individual and as a literary artist reached considerable proportions. Gatsby was reissued with a laudatory introduction by Lionel Trilling, and full-length studies soon were appearing, together with critical anthologies and many articles in both the scholarly and "middlebrow" magazines. Most of the significant criticism on Fitzgerald, indeed, is a product of the last two decades; his works have been reprinted in both softback and hard-cover editions; his stories and novels-especially *The Great Gatsby*-have been "rediscoverered" by academic and non-academic readers throughout the United States and many other countries.

Wherever there is an interest in American literature, the work of F. Scott Fitzgerald has at last "come into its own," and the process is by no means completed. For if a writer like Ernest Hemingway achieved his literary success by eliminating social complexities and "confronting" only those experiences which could be mastered through direct action and ritualized response, one might say that F. Scott Fitzgerald made a success out of "failure" itself. And in the last analysis, we may well wonder which of these two writers has more to tell us of our culture, and our heritage.

THE GREAT GATSBY

ESSAY QUESTIONS AND ANSWERS

. . . .

Question: Discuss the meaning of Idealistic or "non-material" materialism in *The Great Gatsby*.

Answer: Idealistic or "non-material" materialism refers to the fact that for Jay Gatsby, materialism is raised to a romantic ideal, a kind of glowing expectation of some vague and magic "happiness" to be obtained through materialism itself. The paradox, of course, is that idealized materialism "promises" what it can never provide: that is, a spiritual glory. In the person of Jay Gatsby we have a dramatic representation of the uniquely romantic materialism of America, a king of innocence according to which men attempt to create a glowing Ideal from material acquisition, and attempt to convince themselves that desire can define reality, that gesture can define action, and that sentiment can define emotion.

Question: Explain *The Great Gatsby* as a novel with a "dual hero."

Answer: *The Great Gatsby* is a novel with a "dual hero" because Nick Carroway, the narrator, is in many respects no less important to the book than is Jay Gatsby himself. Nick, indeed, represents at least an awareness of the traditional values and moral codes that made America great. A spectator rather than inhabitant of the moral Wasteland of the Buchanan world, Nick provides a definition-through-contrast of the wasteland itself. He also serves as a means of defining the essential idealism of Jay Gatsby, and the waste of energy and devotion which Gatsby's "worship" of Daisy represents.

Question: In what way does Daisy Buchanan represent "the Fitzgerald woman?"

Answer: Daisy Buchanan, whose voice "is full of money," is one of a long line of Fitzgerald women who are both idealized for their beauty, and feared because of their fatal irresponsibility, their parasitism, their lack of any personal substance, and their destructively "romantic" commitment to mere gesture. Daisy, indeed, is a kind of gorgeous "balloon" of loveliness - but a balloon, after all, is a charming surface surrounding empty space. Just so does Daisy "drift" in and out of "love"; lacking any authentic impulse of her own, Daisy is essentially frigid despite (or because of) "her romanticism," She moves, or rather is impelled, in the direction of whatever force-whether of personality or money - seems "in control" at the moment. A creature without loyalty or moral responsibility she is indeed a "Fairy Princess" who belongs to anyone with the proper magic wand.

Question: What is the significance of the billboard face of Doctor T. J. Eckleburg?

Answer: The huge face of Doctor Eckleburg is a kind of presiding deity of the Wasteland. Doctor Eckleburg's stating yellow eyes, indeed, are mistaken for "the eyes of God" by the hapless George Wilson. The billboard is a basic - and extraordinarily provocative-image, a dramatic **parody** of a moral and spiritual Wasteland lost both to the affirmation of God and the affirmation of man.

Question: Discuss the significance of Gatsby's "diary."

Answer: The excerpt from the diary of Jay Gatsby-written while he was still a boy named Jimmy Gatz-is a dramatization of the decay of the American Dream. For the excerpt, shown to Nick by Gatsby's father, is filled with Franklin-like plans for earnest "self-improvement" and hard work. The diary, in short, reinforces a basic **theme** of the novel: the theme of wasted devotion, wasted power, and wasted potential.

Question: *The Great Gatsby* has often been considered a **parody** of "The American Dream." Discuss this concept.

Answer: The "American Dream" is a kind of romantic expectation, a belief in the possibility of achieving some sort of glowing future with hard work and sincere devotion. Fitzgerald's novel is a "**parody**" of this dream, because in the person of Jay Gatsby we have the corruption of the Dream itself: that is, the traditional devotions wasted on spiritual gum-drops and material trivialities.

The American Dream, in short, becomes corrupted into the moral Wasteland of the Buchanans on one hand (a wasteland where impulse and appetite replace moral code and spiritual value), and diluted into the unfocused romanticism of Jay Gatsby on the other. The **parody**, in other words, is created by the fact that Gatsby serves the "vast, vulgar, meretricious beauty" represented by Daisy Buchanan through the modes, and even the gestures, of the American Dream itself. It is for this reason that Nick, at the end of the novel, makes an implicit comparison between Gatsby and the early explorers of the New World. Gatsby too is a man of ideals and self-sacrifice; both the ideals and the sacrifice, however, in the Wasteland lead only to absurd illusion: the worship of Daisy Buchanan, the silver "balloon" of surface without substance.

BIBLIOGRAPHY

GENERAL BACKGROUND

Allen, Frederick Lewis. *The Big Change*. New York, 1952.

Cowley, Malcolm. *Exile's Return*. New York, 1961.

Callaghan, Morley. *That Summer in Paris*. New York, 1963.

Hemingway, Ernest. *A Moveable Feast*. New York, 1963.

May, Henry F. *The End of American Innocence*. New York, 1959.

Munson, Gorham. "The Fledgling Years, 1916-1924," *Sewanee Review* XL (1932), 24-34.

Powers, J.F. "Cross Country-St. Paul, Home of the Saints," *Partisan Review* (July, 1949), 714-21.

Wilson, Edmund., ed. *The Crack-Up*. New York, 1945.

CRITICISM AND LITERARY HISTORY

Beach, Joseph Warren. *American Fiction, 1920-1940*. New York, 1941.

Bewley, Marius. *The Eccentric Design.* New York, 1959.

Bishop, John Peale. *Collected Essays of John Peale Bishop,* ed. Edmund Wilson. New York, 1948.

Burgum, Edwin Berry. *The Novel and the World's Dilemma.* New York, 1947.

Chase, Richard. *The Modern Novel and its Tradition.* New York, 1952.

Daiches, David. *The Novel and the Modern World.* New York, 1940.

Fiedler, Leslie. *Love and Death in the American Novel.* Cleveland, 1962.

Geismar, Maxwell. *The Last of the Provincials.* Boston, 1947.

Hoffman, Frederick J. *The Twenties: American Writing In the Postwar Decade.* New York, 1955.

Kazin, Alfred. *On Native Grounds.* New York, 1942.

Millgate, Michael, *American Social Fiction: James to Cozzens.* New York, 1964.

Mizener, Arthur. *The Sense of Life in the Modern Novel.* Boston, 1964.

Muller, Herbert J. *Modern Fiction: A Study in Values.* New York, 1937.

Savage, D. S. *The Withered Branch: Six Studies in the Modern Novel.* London, 1950.

Snell, George. *The Shapers of American Fiction.* New York, 1947.

Thorp, Willard. *American Writing in the Twentieth Century.* Cambridge, 1960.

Wagenknecht, Edward. *Cavalcade of the American Novel.* New York, 1952.

STUDIES AND CRITICAL ANTHOLOGIES ON F. SCOTT FITZGERALD

Eble, Kenneth E. *F. Scott Fitzgerald*. New York, 1963.

Goldhurst, William. *F. Scott Fitzgerald and his Contemporaries*. Cleveland, 1963.

Kazin, Alfred, ed. *F. Scott Fitzgerald: The Man and his Work*. New York, 1962. (a critical anthology).

Miller, James E. *The Fictional Technique of F. Scott Fitzgerald*. The Hague, 1957.

Mizener, Arthur. *The Far Side of Paradise*. Boston, 1951.

Turnbull, Andrew. *F. Scott Fitzgerald*. New York, 1962.

PERIODICAL ESSAYS AND ARTICLES

For an excellent check list of Fitzgerald criticism see the Spring, 1961 issue of *Modern Fiction Studies*. The attention of the student is drawn to the fact that articles in periodicals are an extremely useful and perhaps major source of Fitzgerald criticism. The check list in *Modern Fiction Studies*, and the collection of critical articles noted above (edited by Mizener and Kazin) are very useful secondary reading. Additional suggestions follow:

Barrett, William. "Fitzgerald and America," *Partisan Review* XVIII (May-June, 1951), 345-353.

Bedingfield, Dolores. "Fitzgerald's Corruptible Dream," *Dalhousie Review* XLI (Winter, 1961-62), 513-521.

Bicknell, John W. "The Wasteland of F. Scott Fitzgerald," *Virginia Quarterly Review* XXX (Autumn, 1954), 556-572.

Cardwell, Guy A. "The Lyric World of F. Scott Fitzgerald," *Virginia Quarterly Review* XXXVIII (Spring, 1962), 162-167.

Freidrich, Otto. "F. Scott Fitzgerald: Money, Money, Money," *American Scholar* XXIX (Summer, 1960), 392-405.

Frohock, W.M. "Morals, Manners, and Scott Fitzgerald," *Southwest Review* 40 (Summer, 1955), 220-228.

Fussell, Edwin. "Fitzgerald's Brave New World," *English Literary History* XIX (December, 1952), 291-306.

Hauserman, H.W. "Fitzgerald's Religious Sense," *Modern Fiction Studies* II (Winter, 1956), 81-82.

Jacobsen, Dan. "F. Scott Fitzgerald," *Encounter* XIV (June, 1960), 71-77.

Lubell, Albert J. "The Fitzgerald Revival," *South Atlantic Quarterly* LIV (January, 1955), 95-106.

Mizener, Arthur. "Scott Fitzgerald and the Imaginative Possession of American Life," *Sewanee Review* LIV (Winter, 1946), 66-86.

_____ "Scott Fitzgerald and the 'Top Girl'," *Atlantic Monthly* CCVII (March, 1961), 56.

Troy, William. "The Authority of Failure," *Accent* VI (Autumn, 1945), 56-60.

CPSIA information can be obtained
at www.ICGtesting.com
Printed in the USA
LVHW051500240821
695994LV00015B/714

9 781645 421283